Those Amazing Tables

Teaching Multiplication

Through Patterns and Color Strips

by Joe Lieberman

Cuisenaire Company of America, Inc.
10 Bank Street. P.O. Box 5026
White Plains, NY 10602-5026

Author's Comments

For many years, I have demonstrated these intriguing, yet little known qualities, of the age-old multiplication tables. Students and teachers invariably respond with surprise and delight. I wish to express thanks to the many teachers in every part of the country who have encouraged me and made suggestions in this endeavor.

Our traditional tables are loaded with surprises for many levels of mathematics learning. These range among place value, number series and patterns, geometric designs and polygons, factors, multiples, common multiples, common factors, equivalent fractions, common denominators, and arithmetic generalizations which, of course, yield algebraic relationships.

The first and foremost of these topics for all teachers is place value. The age-old failure of students in this topic haunts both students and teachers in all later mathematics. The treatment of place value via colors assigned to each place, and the intriguing *on table* method of multiplying with colors promotes student involvement and mastery of both concept and skill.

In these pages lies an opportunity for students to learn the concept behind the multiplication tables, the place value upon which our number system and all computations are based, and the essential relatedness of multiplication to a myriad of other mathematical topics. Without a solid foundation in multiplication concepts and skills, the student suffers continued and increasing deprivation in learning mathematics.

How many generations of us teachers from sixth grade through college have bemoaned this lack of preparation in what is after all—multiplication—not so simple.

Joe Lieberman

ISBN 0-914040-98-7
Permission is granted for limited reproduction of pages
from this book for classroom use.

Printed in U.S.A.

1 2 3 4 5 6 7 8 9 10 - BK-97 96 95 94

Contents

Building Tables

1. The table below has column numbers that run down the table, and row numbers that run across. Look at column 2. As we go down the column, numbers increase by two each time.

   What number should be placed in the square below eight? _____
   Fill in the remaining squares in column 2.

2. Look at column 3 on the table. Numbers in this column increase by three each time.

   What number should be placed in the square below nine? _____
   Fill in the remaining squares in column 3.

3. Look at column 4.

   What number should be placed in the square below four? _____
   Fill in the remaining squares in column 4.

4. Fill in all the missing numbers in the columns.
   Each completed column is called a table.

↓ Columns

1	2	3	4	5	6	7	8	9	10	11	12
2	4	6									
3	6	9									
4	8										
5											
6											
7											
8											
9											
10											
11											
12											

R o w s

Note:

Even numbers always end in 0, 2, 4, 6, or 8.

Odd numbers always end in 1, 3, 5, 7, or 9.

5. Circle all odd numbers. What pattern do you see.

1

Odd And Even Numbers

1. Only odd numbers are given below.   Fill in the missing even numbers.

2. Do you see that odd and even numbers alternate in the 3 table?   Which tables have alternating odd and even numbers?

_____

Which tables have only even numbers? _____

Columns

1		3		5		7		9		11	
3		9		15		21		27		33	
5		15		25		35		45		55	
7		21		35		49		63		77	
9		27		45		63		81		99	
11		33		55		77		99		121	

R o w s

3. Cover the numbers in the 4 table. Can you recall all the numbers?

4. Can you recall the numbers for every table?

5. Without looking at the tables above, place the correct numbers in the indicated squares below.   Circle odd numbers and look for pattern.

Columns

	1	2	3	4	5	6
2						•
3					•	
4				•		
5			•			
6	•					
7						

Columns

	1	2	3	4	5	6
2					•	
3				•		
4			•			
5		•				
6						
7						

Columns

	1	2	3	4	5	6
2	•					
3			•			
4				•		
5					•	
6						•
7						

Columns

	1	2	3	4	5	6
2			•			
3				•		
4					•	
5						•
6						
7						

Meaning Of Rows And Columns

1. Numbers at the top of each column tell how much is added each time. Numbers at the beginning of each row tell how many times a number is added. The tables below are partly completed.

Columns Tell How Much is Added

Rows Tell How Many Times

1	2	3	4	5	6	7	8	9	10
2	4			10		14			
3		9			18			27	
4	8	12				28			40
5			20				40		
6		18			36			54	
7				35			56		
8	16								80
9			36			63			
10		30							

Answer these questions:

10 is a name for 2 times _____

20 is a name for 5 times _____

9 is a name for 3 times _____

35 is a name for 7 times _____

18 is a name for 6 times _____

40 is a name for 5 times _____

54 is a name for 6 times _____

36 is a name for 9 times _____

36 is a name for 6 times _____

63 is a name for 9 times _____

56 is a name for 7 times _____

2. In each partial table below there is an incorrect number. Circle the wrong number.

Columns

	1	2	3	4	5	6
2				8		
3				12		
4				16		
5				18		
6				24		

Rows

Columns

	1	2	3	4	5	6
2						12
3						18
4						22
5						30
6						36

Rows

Columns

	1	2	3	4	5	6
2			6			
3			9			
4			12			
5			14			
6			18			

Rows

Finding Tables

1. Place all of the numbers below into the 3, 6, or 9 table.

Columns: How Much

1	2	3	4	5	6	7	8	9	10	11	12
2		6									
3											
4											
5											
6		⑱									
7		21									
8											
9											
10											
11											
12											

Rows: How Many Times

Cross out each number as it is placed on the tables.

6	12	18	9
18	36	12	66
21	48	27	36
90	24	15	27
54	18	42	72
72	99	30	45
36	30	54	63
60	33	24	81
			108

2. Circle the numbers that fall into more than one of the three tables.

Finding Tables

1. Place all the numbers below into the 4, 6, or 8 tables.

Columns

	1	2	3	4	5	6	7	8	9	10	11	12
2												
3												
4												
5												
6												
7												
8												
9												
10												
11												
12												

R o w s

2. Cross out each number as it is placed on the table.

8	40	60	48
12	20	66	48
16	32	80	56
12	36	88	64
18	42	36	54
16	24	72	72
24	32	96	
24	40	28	
30	48	44	

3. Circle the numbers that fall into more than one of the three tables.

Row Numbers Times Column Numbers

Columns

	1	2	3	4	5	6	7	8	9	10	11	12
2												
3								24				36
4							28	32				
5									45			
6			24				42	48				
7		21							63			
8			32				56					
9		27		45				72				
10											110	
11						66						
12			48									

R o w s

---

1. Fill in the missing column below.

Row	Column	
3 times	_____	= 24
4 times	_____	= 32
6 times	_____	= 42
7 times	_____	= 21
8 times	_____	= 32
9 times	_____	= 27

Row	Column	
10 times	_____	= 110
11 times	_____	= 66
12 times	_____	= 48
3 times	_____	= 36
4 times	_____	= 28
5 times	_____	= 45

Row	Column	
6 times	_____	= 24
6 times	_____	= 48
7 times	_____	= 63
8 times	_____	= 56
9 times	_____	= 45
9 times	_____	= 72

Finding Products

The number at the intersection of a row and column is called a product.   The number 12 is the product of 4 times 3.   Another way to write the product 4 times 3 is: $4 \times 3 = 12$.

1. Complete the products below and fill in the table with the product numbers for all intersecting rows and columns.

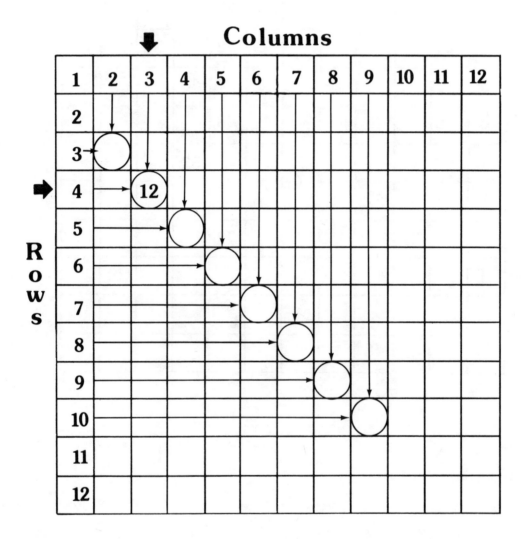

$3 \times 2 =$ _____

$4 \times 3 \ = \ \underline{\ \ 12\ \ }$

$5 \times 4 =$ _____

$6 \times 5 =$ _____

$7 \times 6 =$ _____

$8 \times 7 =$ _____

$9 \times 8 =$ _____

$10 \times 9 =$ _____

A Design Of Squares

Remember: A product is where a row and column cross.

Columns

1	2	3	4	5	6	7	8	9	10	11	12
2											
3											
4											
5											
6											
7											
8											
9											
10											
11											
12											

R o w s

1. Find the answers to the products below.

   $6 \times 1 =$ _____ $9 \times 5 =$ _____ $5 \times 8 =$ _____

   $9 \times 3 =$ _____ $5 \times 6 =$ _____ $9 \times 8 =$ _____

   $2 \times 4 =$ _____ $2 \times 7 =$ _____ $8 \times 10 =$ _____

   $6 \times 4 =$ _____ $12 \times 7 =$ _____ $5 \times 11 =$ _____

2. Place your answers in the correct tables.   A design of three squares can be made by connecting the products.   Can you find it?

Hint: The products are each placed at the corner of a square.

A Table Drawing

1. Find the answers to the products below.   Place a dot in the correct table for each product.

Columns

	1	2	3	4	5	6	7	8	9	10	11	12
2							Start					
3												
4												
5												
6												
7												
8												
9												
10												
11												
12												

Rows

2. Connect the dots.   Each section is a separate line.

$2 \times 4 = \underline{\quad 8 \quad}$	$11 \times 10 = \underline{\qquad}$	$9 \times 5 = \underline{\qquad}$
$5 \times 2 = \underline{\qquad}$	$8 \times 12 = \underline{\qquad}$	$10 \times 6 = \underline{\qquad}$
$8 \times 2 = \underline{\qquad}$	$5 \times 12 = \underline{\qquad}$	$10 \times 7 = \underline{\qquad}$
$11 \times 4 = \underline{\qquad}$	$2 \times 10 = \underline{\qquad}$	$10 \times 8 = \underline{\qquad}$
$12 \times 7 = \underline{\qquad}$	$2 \times 7 = \underline{\qquad}$	$9 \times 9 = \underline{\qquad}$
$7 \times 6 = \underline{\qquad}$	$5 \times 8 = \underline{\qquad}$	$5 \times 4 = \underline{\qquad}$
$8 \times 7 = \underline{\qquad}$	$4 \times 9 = \underline{\qquad}$	$4 \times 5 = \underline{\qquad}$
$7 \times 8 = \underline{\qquad}$	$5 \times 10 = \underline{\qquad}$	$5 \times 6 = \underline{\qquad}$

Is The Answer "Yes"?

1. There is a secret question written in code.

1	2	3	4	5	6	7	8	9	10	11	12
2	B	A	P	W	C	I	F	S	V	U	T
3	F	Z	G	R	K	L	N	D	L	B	G
4	L	I	N	D	J	P	Y	C	M	T	D
5	G	B	M	N	E	G	B	L	V	H	J
6	C	T	U	D	C	X	G	F	D	N	F
7	?	B	K	O	V	K	W	Z	T	F	M
8	Q	P	X	Z	Q	B	F	D	P	D	K
9	D	X	M	K	D	N	C	J	I	X	B
10	I	M	C	J	X	E	M	Z	V	B	L
11	D	F	P	Z	L	D	F	Q	T	P	F
12	G	K	V	S	T	C	M	I	J	C	G

Hidden Question: _____

2. Find the products below. Among the letters in the table, you will find the hidden question.

	Product	Letter
$2 \times 3 =$	6	A
$3 \times 5 =$		
$5 \times 6 =$		
$4 \times 8 =$		
$7 \times 5 =$		
$2 \times 11 =$		

	Product	Letter
$7 \times 8 =$		
$10 \times 2 =$		
$11 \times 10 =$		
$5 \times 11 =$		
$6 \times 4 =$		
$12 \times 5 =$		
$7 \times 2 =$		

Table Designs

Learning is often more interesting and easier when a pattern is found.
Look at the 6 times table below.

1. The 'ones' digits repeat in a pattern:
   6, 2, 8, 4, 0, 6, 2, 8, 4, 0

2. Using a ruler and pencil, draw a line on the
   circle from 6 to 2, then 2 to 8, 8 to 4, 4
   to 0, and 0 back to 6.

3. The name for this figure is a

   _____

1	2	3	4	5	6	7	8
2					12		
3					18		
4					24		
5					30		
6					36		
7					42		
8					48		
9					54		
10					60		

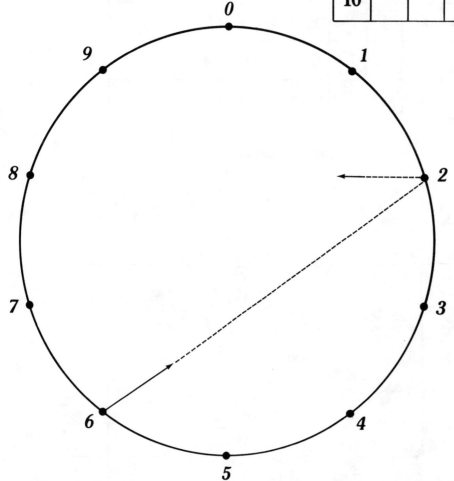

Matching Table Designs

1. The 4 times table also has a pattern and design.

2. The 'ones' digits repeat in the pattern:

   4,_____

3. Using a ruler and pencil, draw a line on the circle from 4 to 8, and then to each digit in the number pattern.

4. The name for this figure is a _____.

1	2	3	4	5	6
2			8		
3			12		
4			16		
5			20		
6			24		
7			28		
8			32		
9			36		
10			40		

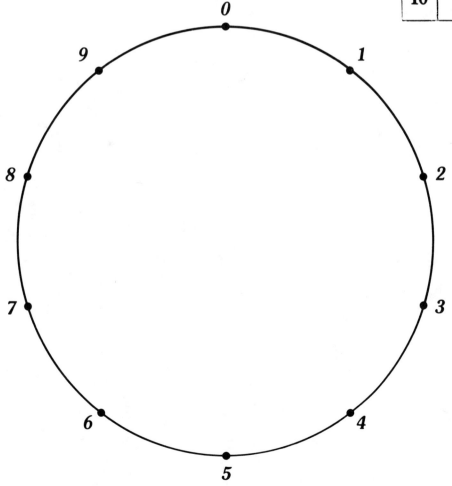

More Table Designs

1. The 'ones' digits in the 8 times table repeat in the pattern:

   8,_____

2. Draw a line on the circle, beginning from 8, to each of the digits of the number pattern in turn.

3. The 4 table (p. 12) has the pattern 4, 8, 2, 6, 0. On the circle below, draw the design of the 4 table again. You may like to use another color.

4. The shape made by the 8 table is a pentagon. After you draw the 4 table design, find a second pentagon and color it.

1	2	3	4	5	6	7	8
2							16
3							24
4							32
5							40
6							48
7							56
8							64
9							72
10							80

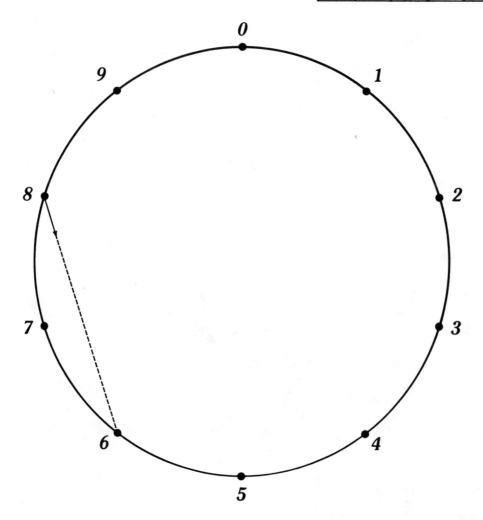

Those Amazing Tables   ©1983 Cuisenaire Company of America

More Matching Designs

1. The 'ones' digits in the 2 times table repeat in the pattern:

   2,_____

2. Draw a line on the circle, beginning from 2, to each of the digits of the number pattern in turn.

3. Draw the 4 table design on the circle again. Use a second color if you like.

4. In addition to the two pentagons and the star, there are three other shapes.   Can you name them?

   _____

   _____

   _____

1	2	3
2	4	
3	6	
4	8	
5	10	
6	12	
7	14	
8	16	
9	18	
10	20	

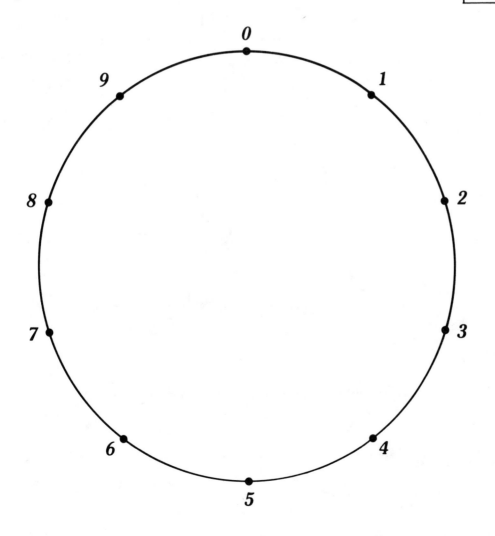

Overlapping Designs

1. The 'ones' digits in the 7 table repeat in a pattern of numbers twice as long as the others you have done. The pattern is:

   7,_____

2. The 'ones' digit number pattern of the 3 table is just as long. The pattern is:

   3,_____

3. Draw a line on the circle from 7 to each of the digits of the pattern in turn. Do the same for the 3 table pattern.

4. Why are the patterns and designs for these tables alike?

1	2	3	4	5	6	7	8
2		6				14	
3		9				21	
4		12				28	
5		15				35	
6		18				42	
7		21				49	
8		24				56	
9		27				63	
10		30				70	
11		33				77	
12		36				84	

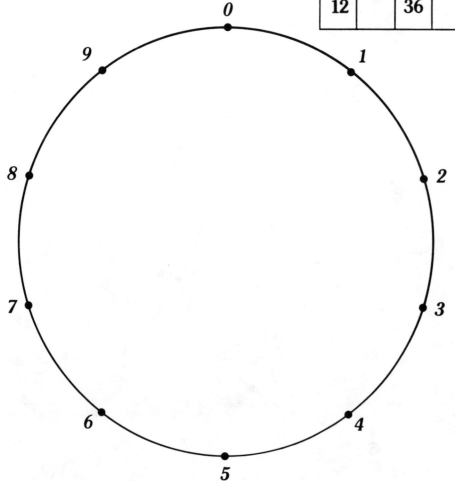

Combining Designs

1. The 'ones' digits in the 9 table repeat in the pattern:

   9, _____

2. Below is the design created by the 7 table or the 3 table. Draw the design for the 9 table using the 'ones' digits of the 9 table pattern.

3. The ten-sided polygon is called a decagon. Find a second decagon and color it.

4. In addition to the two decagons, there are four other shapes. Can you name them?

   _____

   _____

   _____

   _____

1	2	3	4	5	6	7	8	9
2								18
3								27
4								36
5								45
6								54
7								63
8								72
9								81
10								90

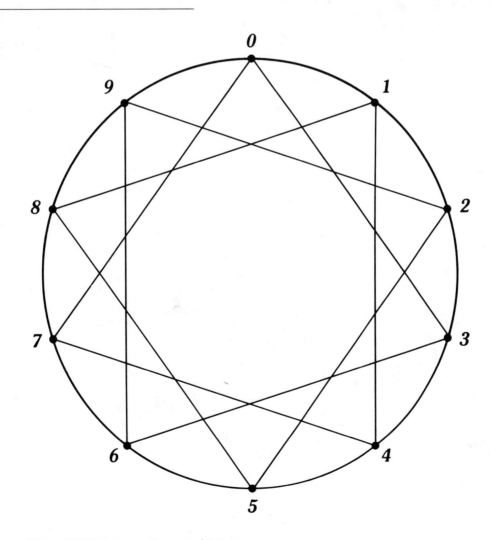

Making Rectangles

1. Column numbers and row numbers form rectangles. Column numbers form one side, and row numbers form another.

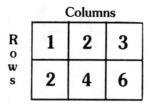

Example:
2 rows by 3 columns form a rectangle 2 by 3.

2. The numbers inside the rectangle are helpful. The largest number in the bottom, right corner counts the number of squares in the rectangle. **For example:**

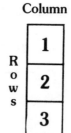
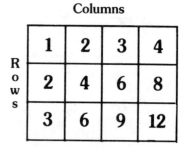

2 rows by 4 columns
8 squares

3 rows by 1 column
3 squares

3 rows by 4 columns
12 squares

3. Complete the partial tables below. Circle the number that tells how many squares are inside each rectangle.

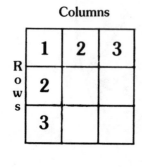
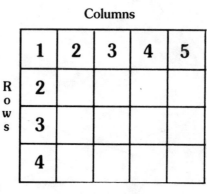

_____ rows by _____ columns

_____ squares

_____ rows by _____ columns

_____ squares

_____ rows by _____ columns

_____ squares

Writing About Rectangles

Here is another way to look at rectangles.   In the example below, there are 2 sets of 3 squares in a 2 by 3 rectangle.

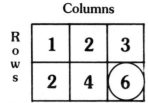

Columns

R o w s	1	2	3
	2	4	⑥

$2 \times 3 = 6$ or $\begin{array}{r} 3 \\ \times\, 2 \\ \hline 6 \end{array}$

"Two times three equals six"

Fill in each circle below and write the multiplication fact.

1.

   | 1 | 2 | 3 | ④ |

   $\underline{1} \times \underline{4} \times = \underline{4}$

2.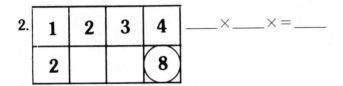

1	2	3	4
2			⑧

   ___ × ___ × = ___

3.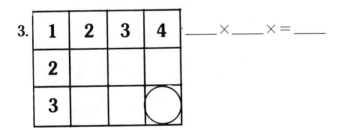

1	2	3	4
2			
3			◯

   ___ × ___ × = ___

4.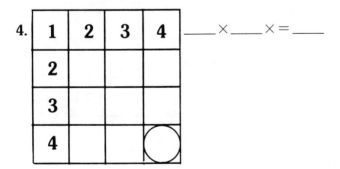

1	2	3	4
2			
3			
4			◯

   ___ × ___ × = ___

5.
1	2	3	4
2			
3			
4			
5			◯

   ___ × ___ × = ___

6.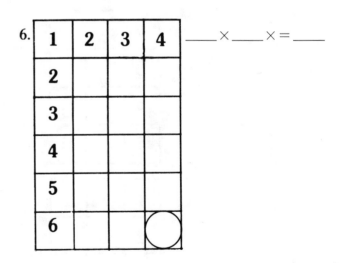

1	2	3	4
2			
3			
4			
5			
6			◯

   ___ × ___ × = ___

Building Tables From Rectangles

Rectangles help to build multiplication tables.   Here are rectangles to show 1 times 3 up to 6 times 3.

1 time

1	2	③

$1 \times 3 = 3$

2 times

1	2	3
2		⑥

$2 \times 3 = 6$

3 times

1	2	3
2		
3		⑨

$3 \times 3 = 9$

4 times

1	2	3
2		
3		
4		⑫

$4 \times 3 = 12$

5 times

1	2	3
2		
3		
4		
5		⑮

$5 \times 3 = 15$

6 times

1	2	3
2		
3		
4		
5		
6		⑱

$6 \times 3 = 18$

Here's a way to show all the rectangles together.

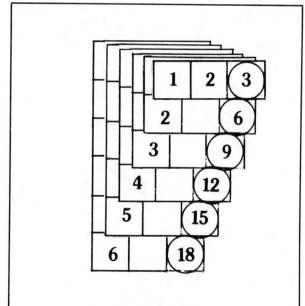

Staple them together to form:

1	2	③
2		⑥
3		⑨
4		⑫
5		⑮
6		⑱

Cut out the six rectangles and try it!

Those Amazing Tables   ©1983 Cuisenaire Company of America

Building Tables From Rectangles

1. Cut out all the rectangles.

2. Put them all together to form the 5 times tables.

1	2	3	4	(5)

1	2	3	4	5
2				(10)

1	2	3	4	5
2				
3				(15)

1	2	3	4	5
2				
3				
4				(20)

1	2	3	4	5
2				
3				
4				
5				(25)

1	2	3	4	5
2				
3				
4				
5				
6				(30)

1	2	3	4	5
2				
3				
4				
5				
6				
7				(35)

1	2	3	4	5
2				
3				
4				
5				
6				
7				
8				(40)

1	2	3	4	5
2				
3				
4				
5				
6				
7				
8				
9				(45)

1	2	3	4	5
2				
3				
4				
5				
6				
7				
8				
9				
10				(50)

1	2	3	4	5
2				
3				
4				
5				
6				
7				
8				
9				
10				
11				(55)

Finding Products From Rectangles

1. Rectangles also help to show how some products relate to others.   Draw a dark line around the rectangles formed by the products in the table below. $1 \times 10 = 10$ is already done.

1	2	3	4	5	6	7	8	9	10	11	12
2	4	6	8	10	12	14	16	18	20	22	24
3	6	9	12	15	18	21	24	27	30	33	36
4	8	12	16	20	24	28	32	36	40	44	48
5	10	15	20	25	30	35	40	45	50	55	60
6	12	18	24	30	36	42	48	54	60	66	72
7	14	21	28	35	42	49	56	63	70	77	84
8	16	24	32	40	48	56	64	72	80	88	96
9	18	27	36	45	54	63	72	81	90	99	108
10	20	30	40	50	60	70	80	90	100	110	120
11	22	33	44	55	66	77	88	99	110	121	132
12	24	36	48	60	72	84	96	108	120	132	144

2. Name the rectangles drawn.

    __1__ × __10__ = 10   _____ × _____ = 10

    _____ × _____ = 10   _____ × _____ = 10

3. How are the rectangles alike?_____

4. Are the circled products in the bottom, right corner of each rectangle? _____

Identical Rectangles

1. For every rectangle that is horizontal, there is another identical vertical rectangle. See two rectangles for the product 12 below.

2. Find four rectangles for the product 18 and draw them on the table.

1	2	3	4	5	6	7	8	9	10	11	12
2	4	6	8	10	12	14	16	18	20	22	24
3	6	9	12	15	18	21	24	27	30	33	36
4	8	12	16	20	24	28	32	36	40	44	48
5	10	15	20	25	30	35	40	45	50	55	60
6	12	18	24	30	36	42	48	54	60	66	72
7	14	21	28	35	42	49	56	63	70	77	84
8	16	24	32	40	48	56	64	72	80	88	96
9	18	27	36	45	54	63	72	81	90	99	108
10	20	30	40	50	60	70	80	90	100	110	120
11	22	33	44	55	66	77	88	99	110	121	132
12	24	36	48	60	72	84	96	108	120	132	144

3. Find two rectangles for the product 54 and draw them on the table.

4. Numbers being multiplied are called factors. Look in the lower left corner of each rectangle to find the factors.

5. Name the two factors of 12 which we used: _____ and _____.

6. We used which two factors of 54? _____ and _____.

7. Name the four factors of 18 which we used: _____, _____, _____, and _____.

Rectangles And Factors

1. The product 12 will appear as six rectangles in the table below.   Find them and draw them.

1	2	3	4	5	6	7	8	9	10	11	12
2	4	6	8	10	12	14	16	18	20	22	24
3	6	9	12	15	18	21	24	27	30	33	36
4	8	12	16	20	24	28	32	36	40	44	48
5	10	15	20	25	30	35	40	45	50	55	60
6	12	18	24	30	36	42	48	54	60	66	72
7	14	21	28	35	42	49	56	63	70	77	84
8	16	24	32	40	48	56	64	72	80	88	96
9	18	27	36	45	54	63	72	81	90	99	108
10	20	30	40	50	60	70	80	90	100	110	120
11	22	33	44	55	66	77	88	99	110	121	132
12	24	36	48	60	72	84	96	108	120	132	144

2. The row numbers used to make the 12 rectangles are called factors of 12.   It is easy to find them in the lower left corner of each rectangle.

   The factors of 12 are _____, _____, _____, _____, _____, and _____.

3. Name the factors for each number than can be shown on the table above.

Product	Factors	Product	Factors
30	3, 5, 6, 10	48	
36		54	
40		63	
42		72	

Rectangles And Factors

1. The product 24 should appear as six rectangles in the table below.   Find them and draw them.

1	2	3	4	5	6	7	8	9	10	11	12
2	4	6	8	10	12	14	16	18	20	22	24
3	6	9	12	15	18	21	24	27	30	33	36
4	8	12	16	20	24	28	32	36	40	44	48
5	10	15	20	25	30	35	40	45	50	55	60
6	12	18	24	30	36	42	48	54	60	66	72
7	14	21	28	35	42	49	56	63	70	77	84
8	16	24	32	40	48	56	64	72	80	88	96
9	18	27	36	45	54	63	72	81	90	99	108
10	20	30	40	50	60	70	80	90	100	110	120
11	22	33	44	55	66	77	88	99	110	121	132
12	24	36	48	60	72	84	96	108	120	132	144

2. If the table above were 24 rows by 24 columns, we could draw two more rectangles for the product 24. These are how long and how wide?

  _____ by _____.

3. List the eight factors of 24. _____, _____, _____, _____, _____, _____, _____, _____.

4. Name the factors for each number that can be shown on the table above.

Product	Factors		Product	Factors
48			81	
56			64	
45			84	

Area Of Rectangles

1. The area of each rectangle is simply the count of the squares inside.

1	2	3
2		

The area of this 2 × 3 rectangle is 6.
Do you see this is the same as finding the product?

1	2	3	4	5
2				
3				

The area of this 3 × 5 rectangle is _____.

1	2	3	4	5	6	7	8	9	10	11	12
2											
3											
4											
5											
6											
7											
8											
9											
10											
11											
12											

2. Find the area of each of these rectangles.

Row	×	Column	Area
1	×	12	_____
2	×	6	_____
3	×	4	_____
4	×	3	_____
6	×	2	_____
12	×	1	_____

3. Find the area of:

Row	×	Column	Area
9	×	7	_____
6	×	8	_____
7	×	8	_____
5	×	9	_____

Those Amazing Tables   © 1983 Cuisenaire Company of America

Perimeters Of Rectangles

The perimeter (distance around) is found by adding the four sides that make a "fence" around the rectangle.

1	2	3	4
2			
3			

Look at the 3×4 rectangle. The perimeter is $3 + 4 + 3 + 4$. Begin at one corner and add the sides all around until you return to where you began.

The perimeter of the 3×4 rectangle is _____.

1	2	3	4	5	6	7	8	9
2								
3								
4								

1. The perimeter of the 4×9 rectangle is

_____.

1	2	3	4	5	6	7	8	9	10	11	12
2	4	6	8	10	12						
3	6	9	12								
4	8	12									
5	10										
6	12										
7											
8											
9											
10											
11											
12											

2. Find the perimeters of each rectangle.

	Perimeter
1×12	_____
2×6	_____
3×4	_____
4×3	_____
6×2	_____
12×1	_____

3. Which has the largest perimeter? _____

4. Which has the smallest perimeter? _____

5. Why? _____

_____

Fences

Imagine that you had a wealthy Texas uncle who has included you in his will.   He has left for you 24 miles of steel fencing to be used on a section of Texas range land shown on the opposite grid paper page. You will be the proud owner of all the Texas land you can fence in with just the 24 miles of fencing.

Let's explore some of the different rectangles you could choose.
Fill out the table below and then draw each rectangle on the opposite page.

Begin each rectangle at Point B

Perimeter	Length	Width	Area
24 miles	11 miles	1 mile	11 square miles
24 miles	10 miles	2 miles	20 square miles
24 miles	9 miles		
24 miles	8 miles		
24 miles	7 miles		
24 miles	6 miles		
24 miles	5 miles		
24 miles	4 miles		

Will all the rectangles use the same total length of fence?_____

What pattern do you see in how the length and width numbers are changing?

_____

Do the number pairs begin to repeat at some point?_____

Which rectangle provides the greatest amount of land? _____

Can you think of a shape which will have even more area, still using the 24 miles of fencing?

_____

Those Amazing Tables   © 1983 Cuisenaire Company of America

Home On The Range

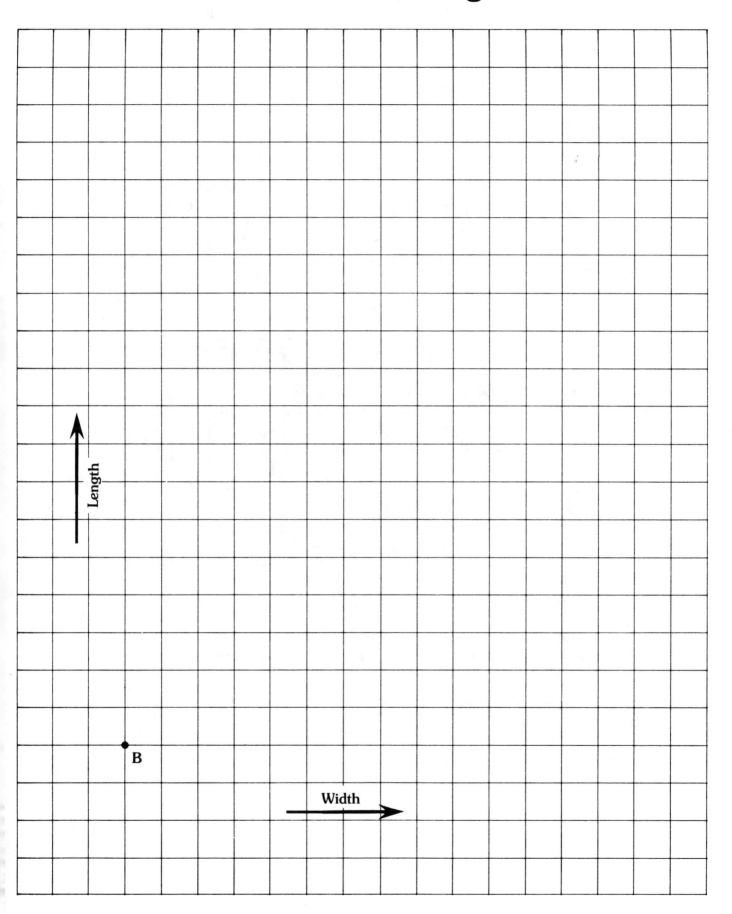

Introducing Color Tables

Times tables are extended when color transparency strips are used.   Take out your yellow strips and try the examples below.   Numbers outside the table help to position the strips.

X	1	2	3	4	5	6	7	8	9	10
1	1	2	3	4	5	6	7	8	9	10
2	2	4	6	8	10	12	14	16	18	20
3	3	6	9	12	15	18	21	24	27	30
4	4	8	12	16	20	24	28	32	36	40
5	5	10	15	20	25	30	35	40	45	50
6	6	12	18	24	30	36	42	48	54	60
7	7	14	21	28	35	42	49	56	63	70
8	8	16	24	32	40	48	56	64	72	80
9	9	18	27	36	45	54	63	72	81	90
10	10	20	30	40	50	60	70	80	90	100

1. Place a yellow strip down the 5 table.   Take another yellow strip and place it across row 3. The two strips intersect at 15, which is the product of 3×5.   Now move the row strip up and down the table to explore the full 5 times table.

2. Move the column strip to other tables, and move the row strip up and down to practice all your times tables.

Those Amazing Tables   © 1983 Cuisenaire Company of America

Mixing Colors

What color do you get when you mix blue and yellow? Well let's find out. Take a blue strip and place it down the 2 column, and take a yellow strip and place it across row 3. Numbers outside the table help to position the strips.

What color appears when you cross blue with yellow? _____

	Column									
X	**1**	**2**	**3**	**4**	**5**	**6**	**7**	**8**	**9**	**10**
1	1	2	3	4	5	6	7	8	9	10
2	2	4	6	8	10	12	14	16	18	20
Row **3**	3	6	9	12	15	18	21	24	27	30
4	4	8	12	16	20	24	28	32	36	40
5	5	10	15	20	25	30	35	40	45	50
6	6	12	18	24	30	36	42	48	54	60
7	7	14	21	28	35	42	49	56	63	70
8	8	16	24	32	40	48	56	64	72	80
9	9	18	27	36	45	54	63	72	81	90
10	10	20	30	40	50	60	70	80	90	100

If the blue strip represents "tens" and the yellow strip "ones", then the cross of 3 times 2 tens (or 20) is equal to 6 "tens", or 60.

Green squares represent the product of "ones" times "tens".

Move the yellow strip up and down the table to find answers to these problems:

$3 \times 20 =$ ___6___ tens, or ___60___

$2 \times 20 =$ _____ tens, or _____

$5 \times 20 =$ _____ tens, or _____

$6 \times 20 =$ _____ tens, or _____

$7 \times 20 =$ _____ tens, or _____

$10 \times 20 =$ _____ tens, or _____

Those Amazing Tables ©1983 Cuisenaire Company of America

A Little Magic

1. The 1 and 2 tables taken together have a little surprise. They repeat the 12 table!

2. Lay a blue strip down the 1 table to represent a column of tens. Lay a yellow strip down the 2 table to represent a column of ones.

3. By laying another yellow strip across | 1 | 2 | , we show the product of 1×10 (a green square), and 1×2 (a yellow square). Thus, 1×12 equals $(1 \times 10) + (1 \times 2)$; or $10 + 2 = 12$.

4. Move the yellow strip down across | 2 | 4 | Can you see 2 tens + 4 ones?

5. Move down to | 4 | 8 | Can you see 4 tens + 8 ones?

6. Move down to | 5 | 10 | Can you see 5 tens + 10 ones?

   The name for this number is _____.

7. Do the following problems using the blue and yellow strips on your table.

Tens	Ones			12 Table
1	2			12
2	4			24
3	6			36
4	8			48
5	10			60
6	12			72
7	14			84
8	16			96
9	18			108
10	20			120
11	22			132
12	24			144

6	12	___6___ tens + ___12___ ones; is really ___72___
7	14	_____ tens + _____ ones; is really _____
8	16	_____ tens + _____ ones; is really _____
9	18	_____ tens + _____ ones; is really _____
10	20	_____ tens + _____ ones; is really _____
11	22	_____ tens + _____ ones; is really _____
12	24	_____ tens + _____ ones; is really _____

31

Those Amazing Tables   ©1983 Cuisenaire Company of America

A Little Magic

1. Look at the 1 and 3 table taken together. Can you see they show the 13 table? Place blue and yellow strips down on the columns as before, with blue on the 1 table and yellow on the 3 table.   Place a yellow strip across

| 1 | | 3 |

to show 1 × 13.

2. Now place the yellow strip across

| 2 | | 6 |

to show 2 × 13; or

20 + 6.   Do you see that the product of ones times tens always appears in the green square?

3. Do the following using the blue and yellow strips on your table:

3 × 13 = | **3** | **9** | _____ tens + _____ ones, or _____

4 × 13 = | **4** | **12** | _____ tens + _____ ones, or _____

5 × 13 = | **5** | **15** | _____ tens + _____ ones, or _____

6 × 13 = | **6** | **18** | _____ tens + _____ ones, or _____

7 × 13 = | **7** | **21** | _____ tens + _____ ones, or _____

8 × 13 = | **8** | **24** | _____ tens + _____ ones, or _____

9 × 13 = | **9** | **27** | _____ tens + _____ ones, or _____

10 × 13 = | **10** | **30** | _____ tens + _____ ones, or _____

11 × 13 = | **11** | **33** | _____ tens + _____ ones, or _____

12 × 13 = | **12** | **36** | _____ tens + _____ ones, or _____

Tens	Ones		13 Table
1	2	3	13
2	4	6	26
3	6	9	39
4	8	12	52
5	10	15	65
6	12	18	78
7	14	21	91
8	16	24	104
9	18	27	117
10	20	30	130
11	22	33	143
12	24	36	156

Practicing Magic Tables

1. Look at the 1 and 6 tables. Complete the 16 table below by using a blue strip to cover the tens column, and yellow strips for ones.

	Tens					Ones
X	1	2	3	4	5	6
1	1	2	3	4	5	6
2	2					12
3	3					18
4	4					24
5	5					30
6	6					36
7	7					42
8	8					48
9	9					54
10	10					60

2. Complete these multiplication facts using color strips and your table.

$1 \times 16 =$ _____ $6 \times 16 =$ _____

$2 \times 16 =$ _____ $7 \times 16 =$ _____

$3 \times 16 =$ _____ $8 \times 16 =$ _____

$4 \times 16 =$ _____ $9 \times 16 =$ _____

$5 \times 16 =$ _____ $10 \times 16 =$ _____

Practicing Magic Tables

1. Here is the complete table for numbers 1 to 10. Use blue and yellow strips to complete the multiplication facts below.

X	1	2	3	4	5	6	7	8	9	10
1	1	2	3	4	5	6	7	8	9	10
2	2	4	6	8	10	12	14	16	18	20
3	3	6	9	12	15	18	21	24	27	30
4	4	8	12	16	20	24	28	32	36	40
5	5	10	15	20	25	30	35	40	45	50
6	6	12	18	24	30	36	42	48	54	60
7	7	14	21	28	35	42	49	56	63	70
8	8	16	24	32	40	48	56	64	72	80
9	9	18	27	36	45	54	63	72	81	90
10	10	20	30	40	50	60	70	80	90	100

$2 \times 14 =$ _____ $3 \times 14 =$ _____

$4 \times 15 =$ _____ $6 \times 17 =$ _____

$7 \times 12 =$ _____ $2 \times 19 =$ _____

$3 \times 18 =$ _____ $1 \times 15 =$ _____

$5 \times 16 =$ _____ $10 \times 16 =$ _____

$9 \times 13 =$ _____ $8 \times 15 =$ _____

Trying Larger Numbers

1. The blue and yellow strips also help us to multiply larger numbers on the table.   Place a blue strip down column 2 and a yellow down column 5.   Take another yellow strip and place it across row 2 to show 2 × 25.

2 × 25 = 4 tens and 10 ones or 50

X	1	2	3	4	5	6	7	8	9	10
1	1	2	3	4	5	6	7	8	9	10
2	2	4	6	8	10	12	14	16	18	20
3	3	6	9	12	15	18	21	24	27	30
4	4	8	12	16	20	24	28	32	36	40
5	5	10	15	20	25	30	35	40	45	50
6	6	12	18	24	30	36	42	48	54	60
7	7	14	21	28	35	42	49	56	63	70
8	8	16	24	32	40	48	56	64	72	80
9	9	18	27	36	45	54	63	72	81	90
10	10	20	30	40	50	60	70	80	90	100

Row 2 labels the second row.

2. Move your yellow row strip up and down the 25 table to complete these multiplication facts.

3. With color strips and the table, products up to 1000 can be found.   Use blue and yellow strips to complete the multiplication facts below.

$2 \times 35 =$ _____ $3 \times 56 =$ _____

$4 \times 48 =$ _____ $5 \times 79 =$ _____

$8 \times 45 =$ _____ $9 \times 36 =$ _____

$7 \times 27 =$ _____ $9 \times 67 =$ _____

$6 \times 78 =$ _____ $9 \times 89 =$ _____

Reversing Tables

1. Look at the table on the opposite page. Can you see that the table below is printed in exactly the reverse order? When the first digit of a two-digit number is larger than the second, we can use this reverse table and the color strips to find products. For example, 3×64 can be found by placing a blue strip down column 6, a yellow strip down column 4, and another yellow strip across row 3.

X	10	9	8	7	6	5	4	3	2	1
1	10	9	8	7	6	5	4	3	2	1
2	20	18	16	14	12	10	8	6	4	2
3	30	27	24	21	18	15	12	9	6	3
4	40	36	32	28	24	20	16	12	8	4
5	50	45	40	35	30	25	20	15	10	5
6	60	54	48	42	36	30	24	18	12	6
7	70	63	56	49	42	35	28	21	14	7
8	80	72	64	56	48	40	32	24	16	8
9	90	81	72	63	54	45	36	27	18	9
10	100	90	80	70	60	50	40	30	20	10

2. Use blue and yellow strips to complete the multiplication facts below.

2×21 _____ 4×82 _____

2×42 _____ 5×53 _____

3×31 _____ 7×41 _____

2×64 _____ 4×92 _____

3×52 _____ 6×75 _____

A Little More Magic

1. The standard multiplication table can be used also with two-digit numbers where the first digit is larger than the second. Instead of using the special reverse table shown on page 36, reverse the position of the color strips on the standard table!

2. Look at the 1 and 2 tables again. This time let's reverse the order and see them as the 21 table. Place a blue strip down the 2 table, and a yellow strip down the 1 table. Now place a yellow strip across to show 1×21.

X	1	2	3
1	1	2	
2	2	4	
3	3	6	
4	4	8	
5	5	10	
6	6	12	
7	7	14	
8	8	16	
9	9	18	
10	10	20	

3. Remember:
The green square shows the product of ones times tens.
The yellow square shows the product of ones times ones.

For 1×21, the green square equals

_____.

Since the location of the tens and ones columns are reversed, the location of the green and yellow squares are reversed!

4. Complete this table

$1 \times 21 = \underline{\ \ 2\ \ }$ tens and $\underline{\ \ 1\ \ }$ ones; or $\underline{\ \ 21\ \ }$ $6 \times 21 = \underline{\hspace{2em}}$ tens and $\underline{\hspace{2em}}$ ones; or $\underline{\hspace{2em}}$

$2 \times 21 = \underline{\hspace{2em}}$ tens and $\underline{\hspace{2em}}$ ones; or $\underline{\hspace{2em}}$ $7 \times 21 = \underline{\hspace{2em}}$ tens and $\underline{\hspace{2em}}$ ones; or $\underline{\hspace{2em}}$

$3 \times 21 = \underline{\hspace{2em}}$ tens and $\underline{\hspace{2em}}$ ones; or $\underline{\hspace{2em}}$ $8 \times 21 = \underline{\hspace{2em}}$ tens and $\underline{\hspace{2em}}$ ones; or $\underline{\hspace{2em}}$

$4 \times 21 = \underline{\hspace{2em}}$ tens and $\underline{\hspace{2em}}$ ones; or $\underline{\hspace{2em}}$ $9 \times 21 = \underline{\hspace{2em}}$ tens and $\underline{\hspace{2em}}$ ones; or $\underline{\hspace{2em}}$

$5 \times 21 = \underline{\hspace{2em}}$ tens and $\underline{\hspace{2em}}$ ones; or $\underline{\hspace{2em}}$ $10 \times 21 = \underline{\hspace{2em}}$ tens and $\underline{\hspace{2em}}$ ones; or $\underline{\hspace{2em}}$

A Little More Magic

1. All of the multiplication facts below can be found using this table and blue and yellow strips.

X	1	2	3	4	5	6	7	8	9	10
1	1	2	3	4	5	6	7	8	9	10
2	2	4	6	8	10	12	14	16	18	20
3	3	6	9	12	15	18	21	24	27	30
4	4	8	12	16	20	24	28	32	36	40
5	5	10	15	20	25	30	35	40	45	50
6	6	12	18	24	30	36	42	48	54	60
7	7	14	21	28	35	42	49	56	63	70
8	8	16	24	32	40	48	56	64	72	80
9	9	18	27	36	45	54	63	72	81	90
10	10	20	30	40	50	60	70	80	90	100

2. Find these products:

$2 \times 42 =$ _____ $1 \times 65 =$ _____

$5 \times 51 =$ _____ $5 \times 34 =$ _____

$3 \times 25 =$ _____ $8 \times 52 =$ _____

$4 \times 75 =$ _____ $10 \times 63 =$ _____

$9 \times 81 =$ _____ $3 \times 16 =$ _____

$7 \times 24 =$ _____ $7 \times 21 =$ _____

$2 \times 84 =$ _____ $10 \times 91 =$ _____

More Than A Little Magic

1. Place blue and yellow strips down the 1 and 3 columns, and horizontally across the 1 and 3 rows as shown on the right.

   There are four intersecting squares as shown below. The "1" is dark blue; the "3's" are green; and the 9 is yellow. The new, blue "hundreds" square represents the product of tens times tens.

   The squares show the partial products of 13 × 13.

	blue		yellow	
blue	1	2	3	4
	2	4	6	8
yellow	3	6	9	12
	4	8	12	16

$$\begin{array}{r} 13 \\ \times\, 13 \\ \hline 9 \\ 30 \\ 30 \\ 100 \\ \hline 169 \end{array}$$

2. Place the blue and yellow strips on the table at the right to show 12 × 12.

   12 × 12 = 1 hundred + 4 tens + 4 ones, or 144

	blue	yellow	
blue	1	2	
yellow	2	4	

3. The bottom table shows 12 × 23. The blue, green, and yellow product squares are

2	3
4	6

   The place value color squares tell us this is

   _____ hundreds + _____ tens + _____ ones; or _____

	blue	yellow
blue	1	2	3
yellow	2	4	6
	3	6	9

More Than A Little Magic

1. Place the blue and yellow strips to show the three color product squares for 23×23.

4	6
6	9

. The hundreds, tens and ones are

_____ hundreds + _____ tens

+ _____ ones

1	2	3	4
2	4	6	8
3	6	9	12
4	8	12	16

Adding the two green squares gives us 12 tens or 120. Thus 23×23 gives:

blue		green		yellow		
400	+	120	+	9	=	529

2. Use the color strips to find the products below.

	Blue		Green		Yellow		Product
$12 \times 34 =$	300	+	100	+	8	=	408
$13 \times 23 =$	_____	+	_____	+	_____	=	_____
$23 \times 23 =$	_____	+	_____	+	_____	=	_____
$13 \times 12 =$	_____	+	_____	+	_____	=	_____
$14 \times 13 =$	_____	+	_____	+	_____	=	_____
$14 \times 23 =$	_____	+	_____	+	_____	=	_____
$14 \times 14 =$	_____	+	_____	+	_____	=	_____
$14 \times 12 =$	_____	+	_____	+	_____	=	_____

Those Amazing Tables   ©1983 Cuisenaire Company of America

More Than A Little Magic

X	1	2	3	4	5	6	7
1	1	2	3	4	5	6	7
2	2	4	6	8	10	12	14
3	3	6	9	12	15	18	21
4	4	8	12	16	20	24	28
5	5	10	15	20	25	30	35
6	6	12	18	24	30	36	42
7	7	14	21	28	35	42	49

1. Use the table and the blue and yellow color strips to practice your multiplication skills.

2. For problems like 32×32, remember to reverse the position of the blue and yellow strips.
   Remember: Yellow squares show ones.
   Green squares show tens.
   Blue squares show hundreds.

	Blue		Green		Yellow		Product
$23 \times 23 =$	_____	+	_____	+	_____	=	_____
$32 \times 32 =$	_____	+	_____	+	_____	=	_____
$32 \times 23 =$	_____	+	_____	+	_____	=	_____
$23 \times 32 =$	_____	+	_____	+	_____	=	_____
$47 \times 23 =$	_____	+	_____	+	_____	=	_____
$74 \times 32 =$	_____	+	_____	+	_____	=	_____
$74 \times 23 =$	_____	+	_____	+	_____	=	_____
$47 \times 32 =$	_____	+	_____	+	_____	=	_____
$17 \times 17 =$	_____	+	_____	+	_____	=	_____
$71 \times 71 =$	_____	+	_____	+	_____	=	_____
$73 \times 17 =$	_____	+	_____	+	_____	=	_____
$17 \times 71 =$	_____	+	_____	+	_____	=	_____

More Than A Little Magic

X	1	2	3	4	5	6	7
1	1	2	3	4	5	6	7
2	2	4	6	8	10	12	14
3	3	6	9	12	15	18	21
4	4	8	12	16	20	24	28
5	5	10	15	20	25	30	35
6	6	12	18	24	30	36	42
7	7	14	21	28	35	42	49

1. Use the table and the blue and yellow color strips
    to practice your multiplication facts.
    Remember: Yellow squares show ones.
    Green squares show tens.
    Blue squares show hundreds.

	Blue		Green		Yellow		Product
23 × 34 =	_____	+	_____	+	_____	=	_____
32 × 43 =	_____	+	_____	+	_____	=	_____
32 × 23 =	_____	+	_____	+	_____	=	_____
23 × 43 =	_____	+	_____	+	_____	=	_____
24 × 24 =	_____	+	_____	+	_____	=	_____
42 × 42 =	_____	+	_____	+	_____	=	_____
42 × 24 =	_____	+	_____	+	_____	=	_____
24 × 42 =	_____	+	_____	+	_____	=	_____
57 × 57 =	_____	+	_____	+	_____	=	_____
75 × 75 =	_____	+	_____	+	_____	=	_____
75 × 57 =	_____	+	_____	+	_____	=	_____
57 × 75 =	_____	+	_____	+	_____	=	_____
47 × 46 =	_____	+	_____	+	_____	=	_____
74 × 64 =	_____	+	_____	+	_____	=	_____
74 × 46 =	_____	+	_____	+	_____	=	_____
47 × 64 =	_____	+	_____	+	_____	=	_____

Place Value Flip-Flop

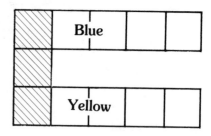

1. Take time to do this carefully.   It will be easier if two students do it together.
   Lay a blue and yellow strip across the table along any rows, but with one open row between them.   Be sure the strips are parallel.   While one student holds them, place a piece of adhesive tape across one end to form a thin shape.   Make two of these.

2. Place the two color ⊟'s on the table to show

	(blue)		(green)		(green)		(yellow)
$13 \times 13 =$	100	+	30	+	30	+	9

3. Flip both ⊟'s over in the same position.   Observe the yellow square (one's place) exchanges position with the dark blue square (hundreds place).
   Do you see from the green 3's and yellow 1 that we are now doing 31×31?

	(blue)		(green)		(green)		(yellow)
$31 \times 31 =$	900	+	30	+	30	+	1

4. Flip the vertical ⊟ back again to show 31×13.   Now all the products change color again!

    $31 \times 13 =$ (blue)   (green)   (green)   (yellow)

    _____ + _____ + _____ + _____

    or _____

5. Once again, flip both ⊟'s from position 4.
   You should now be doing 13×31.

    $13 \times 31 =$ _____ + _____ + _____ + _____

    or _____

1	2	3	4	5
2	4	6	8	10
3	6	9	12	15
4	8	12	16	20
5	10	15	20	25

Place Value Flip-Flop

1. Use the color ⊟'s to find the answer to the multiplication facts on this page.

1	2	3	4	5	6	7	8	9	10
2	4	6	8	10	12	14	16	18	20
3	6	9	12	15	18	21	24	27	30
4	8	12	16	20	24	28	32	36	40
5	10	15	20	25	30	35	40	45	50
6	12	18	24	30	36	42	48	54	60
7	14	21	28	35	42	49	56	63	70
8	16	24	32	40	48	56	64	72	80
9	18	27	36	45	54	63	72	81	90
10	20	30	40	50	60	70	80	90	100

	Blue (100)s		Green (10)s		Yellow (1)s	=	Product
24 × 24	_____	+	_____	+	_____	=	_____
24 × 42	_____	+	_____	+	_____	=	_____
42 × 42	_____	+	_____	+	_____	=	_____
42 × 24	_____	+	_____	+	_____	=	_____
35 × 46	_____	+	_____	+	_____	=	_____
35 × 64	_____	+	_____	+	_____	=	_____
53 × 64	_____	+	_____	+	_____	=	_____
57 × 57	_____	+	_____	+	_____	=	_____
75 × 75	_____	+	_____	+	_____	=	_____

Repeating Digits

1	1	2	2	3	3	4	4
1	1	2	2	3	3	4	4
2	2	4	4	6	6	8	8
2	2	4	4	6	6	8	8
3	3	6	6	9	9	12	12
3	3	6	6	9	9	12	12
4	4	8	8	12	12	16	16
4	4	8	8	12	12	16	16

1. Suppose we wanted to multiply 3×22. The regular times table would require the 2 table to represent both tens and ones. It is much easier if we just print a new table in which every table is printed twice for columns and twice for rows. Place the blue and yellow strips down the 22 columns. Now a yellow strip across row 3 shows 3×22 as 6 tens and 6 ones.

2. Use the color strips to do:

	Blue	Green	Yellow	Product
$4 \times 22 =$	_____ +	_____ +	_____ =	_____
$3 \times 33 =$	_____ +	_____ +	_____ =	_____
$4 \times 33 =$	_____ +	_____ +	_____ =	_____
$3 \times 44 =$	_____ +	_____ +	_____ =	_____
$4 \times 44 =$	_____ +	_____ +	_____ =	_____
$22 \times 11 =$	_____ +	_____ +	_____ =	_____
$44 \times 11 =$	_____ +	_____ +	_____ =	_____
$33 \times 22 =$	_____ +	_____ +	_____ =	_____
$33 \times 33 =$	_____ +	_____ +	_____ =	_____
$40 \times 33 =$	_____ +	_____ +	_____ =	_____
$33 \times 44 =$	_____ +	_____ +	_____ =	_____
$44 \times 44 =$	_____ +	_____ +	_____ =	_____

A complete repeating table for numbers 1 to 10 is printed in the back of this book, and may be used for larger numbers.

One Digit Times Three Digits

1. Place the blue and yellow strips down columns 3 and 5 as before. Take a red strip and place it down column 2. Now place a yellow strip across row 3. The color strips show:

   $3 \times 235 = 600 + 90 + 15$

   The orange square represents the product of ones times hundreds.

2. Move the yellow strip down to row 4. The color strips show:

   $4 \times 235 = 800 + 120 + 20.$

3. Move the yellow strip down to row 6.

   $6 \times 235 = \underline{\hspace{1cm}} + \underline{\hspace{1cm}} +$

   $\underline{\hspace{1cm}}$; or $\underline{\hspace{1cm}}$.

4. Use the color strips to do:

X	Hundreds 1	Tens 2	3	4	Ones 5	6
1	1	2	3	4	5	6
2	2	4	6	8	10	12
3	3	6	9	12	15	18
4	4	8	12	16	20	24
5	5	10	15	20	25	30
6	6	12	18	24	30	36

	Orange	Green	Yellow	Product
$4 \times 246 =$	_____ +	_____ +	_____ =	_____
$5 \times 246 =$	_____ +	_____ +	_____ =	_____
$6 \times 246 =$	_____ +	_____ +	_____ =	_____
$2 \times 345 =$	_____ +	_____ +	_____ =	_____
$3 \times 654 =$	_____ +	_____ +	_____ =	_____
$4 \times 432 =$	_____ +	_____ +	_____ =	_____
$3 \times 531 =$	_____ +	_____ +	_____ =	_____
$5 \times 642 =$	_____ +	_____ +	_____ =	_____

Two Digits Times Three Digits

Multiplication of any and all combinations of digits could be done on the tables with color strips. A special color pattern appears for hundreds as you will see below.

1. For the example 23×234, place vertical red, blue, and yellow strips for 234. Place horizontal blue and yellow strips for 23. **The colored partial products are:**

4	6	8
6	9	12

(We call this a product grid)

The product of ones times ones remains a yellow square.
The product of tens times ones remains a green square.
The product of hundreds times ones will be orange.
The two colors for hundreds products come from 10×10 (blue $\times$ blue), and also 1×100 (yellow $\times$ red). Hundreds will always occur in blue, orange, or both.

The product of hundreds times tens will be a purple square. Thus, thousands are purple.

X	1	2	3	4	5	6	7	8	9
1	1	2	3	4	5	6	7	8	9
2	2	4	6	8	10	12	14	16	18
3	3	6	9	12	15	18	21	24	27
4	4	8	12	16	20	24	28	32	36
5	5	10	15	20	25	30	35	40	45
6	6	12	18	24	30	36	42	48	54
7	7	14	21	28	35	42	49	56	63
8	8	16	24	32	40	48	56	64	72
9	9	18	27	36	45	54	63	72	81

2. Use the color strips to do:

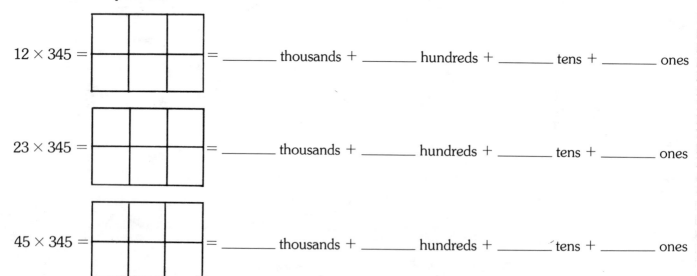

$12 \times 345 =$ ⬚ = _____ thousands + _____ hundreds + _____ tens + _____ ones

$23 \times 345 =$ ⬚ = _____ thousands + _____ hundreds + _____ tens + _____ ones

$45 \times 345 =$ ⬚ = _____ thousands + _____ hundreds + _____ tens + _____ ones

The final answers are 4140, 7935, and 15,525. Did you get them?

Those Amazing Tables   ©1983 Cuisenaire Company of America

Two Digits Times Three Digits

1. Use the color strips to do 13×234.
   Observe the partial products in the colors
   purple, orange and blue, green, and yellow.

X	1	2	3	4	5	6	7	8	9
1	1	2	3	4	5	6	7	8	9
2	2	4	6	8	10	12	14	16	18
3	3	6	9	12	15	18	21	24	27
4	4	8	12	16	20	24	28	32	36
5	5	10	15	20	25	30	35	40	45
6	6	12	18	24	30	36	42	48	54
7	7	14	21	28	35	42	49	56	63
8	8	16	24	32	40	48	56	64	72
9	9	18	27	36	45	54	63	72	81

2. Write these partial products below.

   _____thousands + _____hundreds

   + _____tens + _____ones.

3. Multiply:

   But don't do any place value renaming, e.g., enter 3×4 as 12 and 3×30 as 90 etc.

   $$\begin{array}{r} 234 \\ \times\ 13 \\ \hline 12 \\ 90 \\ 600 \\ -- \\ --- \\ ---- \end{array}$$

4. Now multiply again—this time do the place value renaming as we usually do.   Pay special attention to what you do after you multiply 3×4.

   $$\begin{array}{r} 234 \\ \times\ 13 \\ \hline \end{array}$$

Zero As A Digit

X	1	2	3	4	5	6	7	8	9	10
1	1	2	3	4	5	6	7	8	9	10
2	2	4	6	8	10	12	14	16	18	20
3	3	6	9	12	15	18	21	24	27	30
4	4	8	12	16	20	24	28	32	36	40
5	5	10	15	20	25	30	35	40	45	50
6	6	12	18	24	30	36	42	48	54	60
7	7	14	21	28	35	42	49	56	63	70
8	8	16	24	32	40	48	56	64	72	80
9	9	18	27	36	45	54	63	72	81	90
10	10	20	30	40	50	60	70	80	90	100

1. If a number contains a zero, then one color strip will be missing.   For the number 30, a blue strip will be used, but a yellow will be missing (zero).   The number 70 will use only a blue strip.   Yellow will be missing.

Use the color strips to do:

	(100)s	+	(10)s	+	(1)s	Product	Missing Color Squares
$3 \times 30 =$	_____		_____		_____	_____	_____
$5 \times 30 =$	_____		_____		_____	_____	_____
$8 \times 40 =$	_____		_____		_____	_____	_____
$10 \times 10 =$	_____		_____		_____	_____	_____
$20 \times 20 =$	_____		_____		_____	_____	_____
$20 \times 43 =$	_____		_____		_____	_____	_____
$30 \times 53 =$	_____		_____		_____	_____	_____
$40 \times 53 =$	_____		_____		_____	_____	_____
$90 \times 91 =$	_____		_____		_____	_____	_____
$90 \times 19 =$	_____		_____		_____	_____	_____

Zero As A Digit

X	1	2	3	4	5	6	7	8	9	10
1	1	2	3	4	5	6	7	8	9	10
2	2	4	6	8	10	12	14	16	18	20
3	3	6	9	12	15	18	21	24	27	30
4	4	8	12	16	20	24	28	32	36	40
5	5	10	15	20	25	30	35	40	45	50
6	6	12	18	24	30	36	42	48	54	60
7	7	14	21	28	35	42	49	56	63	70
8	8	16	24	32	40	48	56	64	72	80
9	9	18	27	36	45	54	63	72	81	90
10	10	20	30	40	50	60	70	80	90	100

1. **Remember: If a number contains a zero, then one color strip will be missing.**

   204 will use a red and yellow.   Blue will be missing (zero).

   240 will use a red and _____.   _____ will be missing (zero).

   200 will use a _____.   Both_____

   and _____ will be missing (zeros).

2. Use the color strips to do:

	(1000)s	+	(100)s	+	(10)s	+	(1)s	Product	(Zero) Colors Missing
3 × 200 =	_____		_____		_____		_____	_____	_____
4 × 30 =	_____		_____		_____		_____	_____	_____
3 × 203 =	_____		_____		_____		_____	_____	_____
40 × 30 =	_____		_____		_____		_____	_____	_____
25 × 35 =	_____		_____		_____		_____	_____	_____
25 × 30 =	_____		_____		_____		_____	_____	_____
35 × 300 =	_____		_____		_____		_____	_____	_____
36 × 300 =	_____		_____		_____		_____	_____	_____
35 × 400 =	_____		_____		_____		_____	_____	_____
53 × 400 =	_____		_____		_____		_____	_____	_____
35 × 204 =	_____		_____		_____		_____	_____	_____
73 × 240 =	_____		_____		_____		_____	_____	_____

Multiplication Curves

X	1	2	3	4	5	6	7	8	9	10	11	12
1	1	2	3	4	5	6	7	8	9	10	11	12
2	2	4	6	8	10	12	14	16	18	20	22	24
3	3	6	9	12	15	18	21	24	27	30	33	36
4	4	8	12	16	20	24	28	32	36	40	44	48
5	5	10	15	20	25	30	35	40	45	50	55	60
6	6	12	18	24	30	36	42	48	54	60	66	72
7	7	14	21	28	35	42	49	56	63	70	77	84
8	8	16	24	32	40	48	56	64	72	80	88	96
9	9	18	27	36	45	54	63	72	81	90	99	108
10	10	20	30	40	50	60	70	80	90	100	110	120
11	11	22	33	44	55	66	77	88	99	110	121	132
12	12	24	36	48	60	72	84	96	108	120	132	144

1. Follow the set of 12's on the table as they form a curve.

2. All of the products of a number form curves on the multiplication table. These curves are called hyperbolas.

   They follow a simple rule:

Product =	Row	× Column
	12	1
	6	2
12	4	3
	3	4
	2	6
	1	12

3. We placed two additional dots for guiding our curve; one at the 8th row, and halfway between columns 1 and 2, and the other at the 8th column, and halfway between rows 1 and 2. Use the products of 12 to explain why the curve must go through these two points.

Multiplication Curves

X	1	2	3	4	5	6	7	8	9	10
1	1	2	3	4	5	6	7	8	9	10
2	2	4	6	8	10	12	14	16	18	20
3	3	6	9	12	15	18	21	24	27	30
4	4	8	12	16	20	24	28	32	36	40
5	5	10	15	20	25	30	35	40	45	50
6	6	12	18	24	30	36	42	48	54	60
7	7	14	21	28	35	42	49	56	63	70
8	8	16	24	32	40	48	56	64	72	80
9	9	18	27	36	45	54	63	72	81	90
10	10	20	30	40	50	60	70	80	90	100

1. Locate and enter the products of 10 in the four squares where they belong.

2. Draw a hyperbola curve between these four products. Make the curve go through the two guide dots.

3. List the factors of 10 just as we did for 12 on page 51.

Product = Row × Column

10

_____ × _____

_____ × _____

_____ × _____

_____ × _____

4. The guide dots are at row 4 and column "2½", and column 4 and row "2½".

Why does 4 and 2½ lie on the curve?

Sums of Tables

1. The sum of the products of two tables are equal to a third table. Look at the products in Tables 3, 5, and 8 below.

Look at row 2.
Do you see that 6 + 10 = 16?

Look at row 3.
Do you see that 9 + 15 = 24?

2. Find the missing product in Table 3, Table 5, or Table 8 below. Are the sums of Table 3 and Table 5 always equal to Table 8?

Table 3 + Table 5 = Table 8

15   +_____ =   40

_____ +   15   =   24

18   +_____ =   48

21   +   35   =_____

_____ +   40   =   64

1	2	3	4	5	6	7	8	9	10	11	12
2	4	6	8	10	12	14	16	18	20	22	24
3	6	9	12	15	18	21	24	27	30	33	36
4	8	12	16	20	24	28	32	36	40	44	48
5	10	15	20	25	30	35	40	45	50	55	60
6	12	18	24	30	36	42	48	54	60	66	72
7	14	21	28	35	42	49	56	63	70	77	84
8	16	24	32	40	48	56	64	72	80	88	96
9	18	27	36	45	54	63	72	81	90	99	108
10	20	30	40	50	60	70	80	90	100	110	120
11	22	33	44	55	66	77	88	99	110	121	132
12	24	36	48	60	72	84	96	108	120	132	144

3. Try two other tables whose sum is less than twelve, and find the table equal to their sum.

Sums of Tables

1. The table addition on the previous page can also be expressed through the <u>distributive property</u> of multiplication.

2. One way to write 2 times the sum of tables 4 and 7 is:

    $(2 \times 4) + (2 \times 7) = (2 \times 11)$; or

    $8 + 14 = 22$

    Another way to write the same sum of two products is:

    $2 \times (4 + 7) = (2 \times 11)$; or

    $(2 \times 4) + (2 \times 7) = (2 \times 11)$; or

    $8 + 14 = 22$

1	2	3	4	5	6	7	8	9	10	11	12
2	4	6	8	10	12	14	16	18	20	22	24
3	6	9	12	15	18	21	24	27	30	33	36
4	8	12	16	20	24	28	32	36	40	44	48
5	10	15	20	25	30	35	40	45	50	55	60
6	12	18	24	30	36	42	48	54	60	66	72
7	14	21	28	35	42	49	56	63	70	77	84
8	16	24	32	40	48	56	64	72	80	88	96
9	18	27	36	45	54	63	72	81	90	99	108
10	20	30	40	50	60	70	80	90	100	110	120
11	22	33	44	55	66	77	88	99	110	121	132
12	24	36	48	60	72	84	96	108	120	132	144

3. Fill in the missing row and column numbers. The first example is done for you.

    $2 \times (4 + 7) = (2 \times 11)$ $5 \times (4 + \underline{\ \ }) = (5 \times 11)$

    $(2 \times \underline{4}) + (2 \times \underline{7}) = 22$ $(5 \times \underline{\ \ }) + (5 \times \underline{\ \ }) = 55$

    $3 \times (4 + 7) = (3 \times 11)$ $6 \times (4 + 7) = (6 \times 11)$

    $(3 \times \underline{\ \ }) + (3 \times \underline{\ \ }) = 33$ $(\underline{\ \ } \times 4) + (\underline{\ \ } \times 7) = 66$

    $4 \times (\underline{\ \ } + 7) = (4 \times 11)$

    $(4 \times \underline{\ \ }) + (4 \times \underline{\ \ }) = 44$

Table Powers

1. The word power indicates repeated multiplication of the same factor. For example: 2^3 says 2 to the 3rd power or $2 \times 2 \times 2 = 8$.

	Says	**Means**	**Equals**
3^2	<u>3 to the 2nd power</u>	3×3	9
2^4	_____	$\_ \times \_ \times \_ \times \_$	_____
4^3	_____	$\_ \times \_ \times \_$	_____
3^3	_____	$\_ \times \_ \times \_$	_____
2^5	_____	$\_ \times \_ \times \_ \times \_ \times \_$	_____
3^4	_____	$\_ \times \_ \times \_ \times \_$	_____

2. 2^1 is the same as saying 1×2. Its picture is

1	2

2^1

3. You can see 2^2 by doubling the 1×2 rectangle as shown here.

1	2
2	4

$2^2 = 2^1 \times 2$

4. 2^3 is the 3rd power of 2. It means $2 \times 2 \times 2$.
But 2×2 is 2^2. So $2^3 = 2^2 \times 2$.
All we need do is double the picture for 2^2 to see 2^3.

1	2	3	4
2	4	6	8

$2^3 = 2^2 \times 2$

5. 2^4 is the _____ power of 2.

It equals _____ $\times$ _____ $\times$ _____ $\times$ _____.
But $2 \times 2 \times 2$ is 2^3. So $2^4 = 2^3 \times 2$.

All we need do is _____ the picture of 2^3 to see 2^4.

1	2	3	4
2	4	6	8
3	6	9	12
4	8	12	16

$2^4 = 2^3 \times 2$

6. 2^5 says _____ to the _____ power.

2^5 also equals _____ $\times$ _____ $\times$ _____ $\times$ _____ $\times$ _____.

2^5 also equals _____ $\times 2$.
The picture for 2^5 is double the picture for

_____.

$2^5 = 2^4 \times 2$

1	2	3	4	5	6	7	8
2	4	6	8	10	12	14	16
3	6	9	12	15	18	21	24
4	8	12	16	20	24	28	32

7. 2^6 is not on this page. You will find its picture on the multiplication table.

2^6 is double _____.

More Table Powers

$3^1 = 3$

$3^2 = 3^1 \times 3$

$3^3 = 3 \times 3 \times 3 = 3^2 \times 3$

$3^4 = $ ____ $\times$ ____ $\times$ ____ $\times$ ____ $=$ ____ $\times 3$

$3^5 = $ ____ $\times$ ____ $\times$ ____ $\times$ ____ $\times$ ____ $=$ _____ $\times 3$

3^5 is too big for our 12×12 table.

1	2	3

3^1

1	2	3
2	4	6
3	6	9

$3^2 = 3^1 \times 3$

1	2	3						
2	4	6						
3	6	9			18			27

$3^3 = 3^2 \times 3$

		3						
		9						27
								81

$3^4 = 3^3 \times 3$

		3									
		9									27
											81
											243

$3^5 = 3^4 \times 3$

Those Amazing Tables   ©1983 Cuisenaire Company of America

Times Table Fractions

1. Look at rows 1 and 2 in the table below. Can you see the fractions:

$$\frac{1}{2}, \quad \frac{2}{4}, \quad \frac{3}{6}, \quad \frac{4}{8}, \quad \frac{5}{10}, \quad \frac{6}{12}, \quad \frac{7}{14}, \quad \frac{8}{16}, \quad \frac{9}{18}, \quad \frac{10}{20}, \quad \frac{11}{22}, \quad \frac{12}{24}$$

These are equivalent fractions which means they are all equal in value. Every fraction to the right of ½ is equivalent to ½. The table is filled with sets of equivalent fractions.

2. Can you see the set for $\frac{2}{3}, \quad \frac{3}{4}, \quad \frac{5}{6}, \quad \frac{9}{10}, \quad \frac{?}{},$

Now skip a line or two between the rows.

Find the set of equivalent fractions for:

$$\frac{1}{3}, \quad \text{—}, \quad \text{—}, \quad \text{—}, \quad \frac{5}{15}$$

$$\frac{2}{4}, \quad \text{—}, \quad \text{—}, \quad \text{—}, \quad \frac{10}{20}$$

$$\frac{3}{5}, \quad \text{—}, \quad \text{—}, \quad \text{—}, \quad \frac{15}{25}$$

$$\frac{1}{4}, \quad \text{—}, \quad \text{—}, \quad \text{—}, \quad \frac{5}{20}$$

$$\frac{2}{5}, \quad \text{—}, \quad \text{—}, \quad \text{—}, \quad \frac{10}{25}$$

$$\frac{3}{7}, \quad \text{—}, \quad \text{—}, \quad \text{—}, \quad \frac{15}{35}$$

$$\frac{2}{3}, \quad \text{—}, \quad \text{—}, \quad \text{—}, \quad \frac{10}{15}$$

$$\frac{2}{9}, \quad \text{—}, \quad \text{—}, \quad \text{—}, \quad \frac{10}{45}$$

1	2	3	4	5	6	7	8	9	10	11	12
2	4	6	8	10	12	14	16	18	20	22	24
3	6	9	12	15	18	21	24	27	30	33	36
4	8	12	16	20	24	28	32	36	40	44	48
5	10	15	20	25	30	35	40	45	50	55	60
6	12	18	24	30	36	42	48	54	60	66	72
7	14	21	28	35	42	49	56	63	70	77	84
8	16	24	32	40	48	56	64	72	80	88	96
9	18	27	36	45	54	63	72	81	90	99	108
10	20	30	40	50	60	70	80	90	100	110	120
11	22	33	44	55	66	77	88	99	110	121	132
12	24	36	48	60	72	84	96	108	120	132	144

Changing Terms

1. Look at the rows for $\frac{1}{2}$. The fraction $\frac{6}{12}$ is another name for $\frac{1}{2}$.

   Rename $\frac{1}{2}$ into:

   $\overline{10}$, $\overline{16}$, $\overline{18}$, $\overline{24}$, $\overline{14}$, $\overline{8}$, $\overline{22}$

2. Rename $\frac{2}{3}$ into:

   $\overline{6}$, $\overline{12}$, $\overline{21}$, $\overline{27}$, $\overline{36}$, $\overline{24}$, $\overline{18}$

3. Rename both $\frac{2}{3}$ and $\frac{3}{4}$ as 12th's: $\overline{12}$ and $\overline{12}$

4. Rename both fractions and then add them.

   $$\frac{1}{2} + \frac{1}{3} = \overline{6} + \overline{6} =$$

5. Rename all three and then add them.

   $$\frac{2}{5} + \frac{1}{4} + \frac{3}{10} = \overline{20} + \overline{20} + \overline{20} =$$

6. Look at the set of fractions equivalent to $\frac{2}{3}$. Write every second fraction beginning with $\frac{4}{6}$ in the spaces below.

   $$\frac{4}{6} = \frac{12}{18} = \text{—} = \text{—} = \text{—} = \text{—}$$

7. Write every fraction equivalent to $\frac{4}{5}$ if its denominator ends in 5.

   $$\frac{4}{5} = \text{—} = \text{—} = \text{—} = \text{—} = \text{—}$$

8. Write every fraction equivalent to $\frac{5}{8}$ below.

   $$\frac{5}{8} = \text{—} = \text{—} = \text{—} = \text{—} = \text{—} = \text{—} = \text{—} = \text{—} = \text{—} = \text{—} = \text{—}$$

Those Amazing Tables © 1983 Cuisenaire Company of America

Comments and Answers

Reading Tables

This first section is intended to introduce the tables from the very beginning. Use is made at once of pattern, number design and color to draw students into the material. Completion of the pages in this chapter assumes a reasonably firm foundation in one-digit multiplication, either through initial work in class before the activities in this chapter, or through simultaneous workbook exercises.

Selected Comments

Page 1: **Building Tables**—While this initial worksheet is intended to acquaint students with number patterns for each table, there is also an opportunity to focus on odd and even numbers. Here are some patterns for odd and even numbers:

1. Odd numbers only appear in the 1, 3, 5, 7, 9, and 11 columns and rows.

2. Odd numbers appear in those rows and columns at every other number.

3. Odd numbers increase by 2 in the 1 column, by 6 in the 3 column, by 10 in the 5 column, and so on.

Page 2: **Odd and Even Numbers**—Patterns for odd and even numbers on page 1 are reintroduced here. Activity 5 is intended to give students early practice in memorizing multiplication facts from the table.

Page 3: **Meaning of Rows and Columns**—This page is particularly important for activities throughout the book. Numbers on the table are defined, and multiplication is described in terms of column numbers and row numbers. This definition will be used consistently throughout the book.

Page 7: **Finding Products**—A product is defined as the point of intersection on the table of a row and column. Multiplication will always be shown as row X column in this book. Therefore, commutativity will be later shown as two different rectangular figures, each with the same area. For example, the product of 3 × 4 and 4 × 3 will be shown in two separate locations.

Selected Answers

Page 8: Here are the three squares.

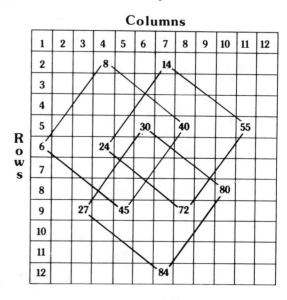

Page 9: The picture is of a pumpkin.

Page 10: Hidden Question: Are you with us?

Table Designs and Patterns

These pages show an example of the unexpected results which reward exploration of table designs based upon the units digits and a ten point circle. These conditions can be changed by students who wish to make their own discoveries. An idea is offered below as an example.

1. The space capsule—connect all the products ending in 2 or 8 on the table.

2. A design of squares—connect all products ending on the table with 5.

3. Rhombus—connect all products ending on the table in 9 or 1.

4. Giant X—connect products ending in 3; then all products ending in 7 on the table.

Selected Answers.

Pp. 11-12: The name for this figure is a star.

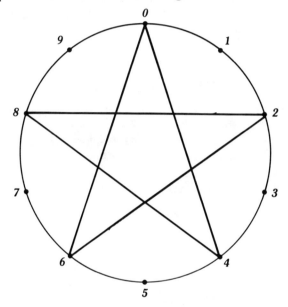

Page 13: The shaded area represents a second pentagon.

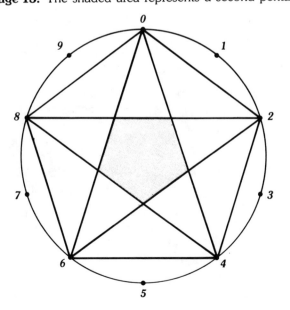

Page 14: Three additional shapes may be: triangles, trapezoids, and parallelograms. Students may also name the rhombus and kite.

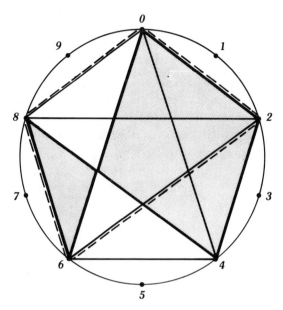

Page 15: By now, students may see that the same pattern occurs for 6 and 4, 8 and 2, and now 7 and 3. Each number pair represents a sum of ten.

Page 16: Four additional shapes are triangles, trapezoids, parallelograms (or rhombuses), and kites.

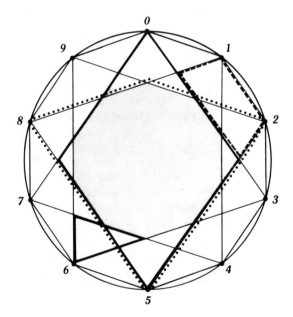

Tables and Rectangles

These pages are essentially based on the concept that the formula for area of rectangles is identical with the table products we are learning. Teachers should point out the symmetry of these rectangles as they are drawn. Coloring of symmetric parts of a design such as that on page 25 can be motivating as well as instructive.

Perimeter is taken as a companion to area. It provides a good jumping-off point to previous study and reinforcement of measurement skills.

Selected Answers

Page 26: Excercises 3 and 4 point out the difference between area and perimeter. While each rectangle has an area of 12 units, the longer, narrow rectangles have a greater perimeter.

Page 27: Exercises 2 through 6 emphasize the difference between area and perimeter by asking students to build rectangles using the same amount of fencing (perimeter 24 miles). Students should note that as a rectangle approaches a square, its area increases. The answer to exercise 6 is "a circle." This experience can be demonstrated by using a piece of string to form all possible shapes with the same perimeter.

Color Tables

The yellow, blue, and red strips are used to designate the place value of numbers in the same way we use zeros in our base ten system. In effect, we have color-coded our zeros.

The result of the color strip designation for place value is a rainbow of colors for the partial products of numbers. The range is from 10^1 (ones times ones) up to 10^4 (hundreds times hundreds) as shown in the Partial Products chart below:

1×1	1×10	10×10
dark yellow	green	dark blue
1×100	10×100	100×100
orange	purple	dark red

Using the intersections of color strips on the multiplication table helps to reinforce two ideas: the product of numbers larger than 9 involves an awareness of place value; and the color designation of each partial product helps children to recognize the value of each partial product when using traditional paper and pencil.

Selected Comments

Page 30: A distinction is made between the designated value of the yellow (ones) and blue (tens) strips, and the resulting product of ones and tens (a green square). The crossing of two colors to create a third is identical to the resulting answer when multiplying ones times tens.

Page 36: There is a magnificent beauty to the order of numbers, and the table helps us to see it. By reversing the table, we are able to deal with multiplication of numbers whose sequence is reversed, i.e., 74 instead of 47. The position of the strips remains unchanged, while the tables have been reversed.

Page 37: There is a certain magic to the discovery that the same table can be used if the strips are reversed, and the author has chosen to continue this model for the remainder of the book. While some may question the efficacy of reversing the position of tens and ones, the intent of these pages is not to teach or to introduce place value, but to dramatize its impact on multiplication through the color strips. When multiplying two binomials, for example 12×13, it is the four partial products, not necessarily the order in which we multiply them that is important.

Table Adventures

On these pages, the reader will find a brief introduction to additional table activities. These are included for students and teachers who might wish to explore the many topics introduced on the table. The color strips continue to be useful in searching for other patterns since they highlight the numbers being observed.

Selected Comments

Pages 51-52: The locations of the same product number on the table will always form a hyperbola. These locations are the positions of ordered pairs. Thus, a relationship exists between the factors of a product and the ordered pairs of the hyperbola. This is true because the formula for the hyperbola is $K=XY$; or a constant is equal to row times column. In this case, the constant is 12 on page 51 and 10 on page 52. The X and Y pairs are of course factors of 12 or 10.

Pages 55-56: These pages will have continuing impact upon the students' basic concepts of powers in later grades. The concept of powers as repeated multiplication is useful, just as the concept of multiplication as repeated addition is initially helpful. One nice feature of this procedure is that it provides a visual image for students.

Pages 57-58: These two pages introduce fractions. This entire topic will be the subject matter of a later book on the use of color strips and tables in a study of fractions.